THE
COLLIE

by Charlotte Wilcox

Consultant:
Virginia Holtz
Co-chairman, Education Committee
Collie Club of America, Inc.

CAPSTONE
HIGH/LOW BOOKS
an imprint of Capstone Press
Mankato, Minnesota

Capstone High/Low Books are published by Capstone Press
818 North Willow Street • Mankato, MN 56001
http://www.capstone-press.com

Library of Congress Cataloging-in-Publication Data
Wilcox, Charlotte.
    The collie/by Charlotte Wilcox.
        p. cm. — (Learning about dogs)
    Includes bibliographical references and index.
    Summary: An introduction to this gentle, intelligent breed of herding dogs,
covering its history, development, habits, and required care.
    ISBN 0-7368-0005-0
    1. Collie—Juvenile literature. [1. Collie. 2. Dogs.] I. Title. II. Series:
Wilcox, Charlotte. Learning about dogs.
SF429.C6W48 1999
636.737'4—dc21
                                                        98-6581
                                                           CIP
                                                            AC

Editorial Credits
Matt Doeden, editor; Timothy Halldin, cover designer; Sheri Gosewisch,
    photo researcher
Photo Credits
Helen Longest-Slaughter, 30, 32
John Springer, Corbis-Bettmann, 18
Kent & Donna Dannen, 13, 22, 25, 28, 35, 40
Mark Raycroft, cover, 4, 6, 10, 26
Thomas R. Fletcher, 14, 17, 39
Unicorn/James L. Fly, 9; Ronald E. Partis, 36
Ward Baldwin/Corbis-Bettmann, 20

Table of Contents

Quick Facts about the Collie

Description

Height:

Collies stand 22 to 26 inches (56 to 66 centimeters) tall. Height is measured from the ground to the withers. The withers are the tops of the shoulders.

Weight:

Collies weigh from 50 to 75 pounds (23 to 34 kilograms).

4

Physical features: Collies can have two types of coats. Rough collies have long coats. Smooth collies have short coats.

Color: Collies are usually a mix of brown, black, gray-blue, or white. Most collies have tan markings on their faces and legs. They often have white markings on their necks, legs, and feet.

Development

Place of origin: Collies came from Scotland and England.

History of breed: Collies came from early European herding dogs. Farmers used these dogs to herd and guard sheep.

Numbers: United States dog clubs register about 12,000 collies each year. Register means to record a dog's breeding record with an official club. Canadian dog clubs register about 1,000 collies each year.

Uses

Most collies in North America are family pets. Some are service dogs that help people who are disabled. Others herd sheep or cattle on farms.

Chapter 1
Gentle Guards

The collie is among the most popular dog breeds in the world. Collies are friendly and intelligent. Their beautiful coats make them popular.

The collie breed began in Scotland. Farmers used early collies to herd animals such as sheep and cattle. These dogs were gentle with sheep and lambs. Collies were fearless guards. They learned to obey people's commands from long distances. Collies understood voice commands and hand signals. Some experienced collies could herd groups of animals by themselves.

Collies' beautiful coats make them popular.

Collies' good nature and intelligence make them good pets today. Most collies get along well with children and other animals. When trained, they obey their owners' commands. Pet collies are good guard dogs. They bark if strangers arrive. But they rarely attack.

Lassie

Most people think of a dog named Lassie when they think of collies. Lassie was a character in books, television shows, and movies.

Lassie first appeared in a magazine story. The dog in the magazine story was smart, brave, and faithful. These characteristics helped Lassie save many lives in the books, television shows, and movies that followed. Real collies have many of the same characteristics as Lassie.

Most collies get along well with children.

Chapter 2

The Beginnings of the Breed

The first collies were mostly black. People called them coally dogs because the dogs' black fur looked like coal. These dogs were smaller than collies are today.

Farm Work

For centuries, collies were farm dogs. They lived mostly in Scotland and northern England. Early collies helped take care of farm animals. The dogs kept animals from wandering away from farms. Collies guarded the animals from wolves.

The first collies were mostly black.

Collies helped farmers herd many types of farm animals. They herded cows, goats, and pigs. Some even herded geese and ducks. Collies seemed to work best with sheep.

Collies and Sheep

Sheep were very important to farmers in Scotland. Farmers raised sheep for wool and for meat. Farmers needed good dogs to care for their sheep. They trained collies for this work.

Collies became well known for herding sheep. They knew how to keep sheep in one place. They also could make sheep move from place to place.

Most collies were farm dogs until the mid-1800s. People built railroads through Scotland then. People from other areas traveled to Scotland on the railroads. Farmers sold some of their collies to these people.

Queen Victoria

Queen Victoria of England visited Scotland in 1860. She liked the farmers' collies. She brought some collies home to her castle. Her

Collies have a special talent for herding sheep.

collies were the first many people in southern
England had ever seen.

Many people wanted to own collies like
Queen Victoria's. Breeders began to raise
collies. People showed their collies in dog
shows. People also found that collies made
good pets.

Chapter 3

The Development of the Breed

Collies' popularity grew during the late 1800s. People wrote stories about collies. The stories introduced people to brave and smart collies. Many people kept collies as pets.

Old Cockie and Charlemagne
Old Cockie was one of the first successful show collies. He was born in England in 1867. Old Cockie was a sable collie. Sable is a shade of brown.

Old Cockie had a famous grandson named Charlemagne (shar-luh-MAYN). Charlemagne

Many people keep collies as pets.

was sable and white. People liked Charlemagne's color pattern. They wanted dogs that looked like him. Many people bought puppies that Charlemagne fathered.

People brought collies to North America in the 1870s. Most came from dogs Charlemagne had fathered. The Collie Club of America began in 1886. The club helped people find and breed healthy collies.

Lad

In 1919, Albert Terhune wrote a book about a collie. The book was *Lad, a Dog*. In the book, Lad risked his life to help a disabled girl.

Terhune wrote other books about collies. Millions of North American readers enjoyed Terhune's stories. Many readers wanted dogs like Lad. The popularity of the collie breed grew.

The Collie Club of America helps people find and breed healthy collies.

In 1943, producers made the movie *Lassie Come Home.*

Lassie Stories

Eric Knight wrote *Lassie Come Home* in 1938. It was the tale of a faithful collie that became separated from her family. In the story, Lassie made a long journey to return to her family. She survived many dangers to return home.

In 1943, producers made the movie *Lassie Come Home.* The producers needed a collie to play the part of Lassie. They wanted a beautiful, well-trained female dog. They began to search for the perfect collie.

Pal

Rudd Weatherwax heard about the producers' search. He had a collie named Pal. Pal was beautiful and well trained. Weatherwax wanted Pal to play the part of Lassie. But Pal was a male.

The movie producers hired a female dog to play the part of Lassie. But they hired Pal to perform the tricks the other dog could not do.

One scene in the movie called for Lassie to swim across a river. The other dog would not swim across the river. The producers had Pal swim instead. Pal jumped into the river and swam hard. He looked very tired when he reached the other side. It was exactly what the producers wanted.

The producers thought Pal was so good they made him Lassie instead. He became a movie star. Most people thought Pal's name was Lassie. Few people knew he was a male.

Pal's Sons

The first *Lassie* movie was successful. The producers made more of them. Pal starred in all of the early Lassie movies. He became most people's idea of the perfect collie.

Producers had a hard time finding other collies that looked like Pal. After Pal died, one of his male offspring took over the part. The dog looked much like Pal.

In 1954, the *Lassie* television show began. One of Pal's offspring played the part of Lassie. Later, more of Pal's offspring played the part. Rudd Weatherwax and his son Robert trained all the dogs that played Lassie.

In 1954, the *Lassie* television show began.

Chapter 4

The Collie Today

Collies are still popular in North America. The American Kennel Club registers more than 12,000 collies each year. The Canadian Kennel Club registers more than 1,000 collies each year. Register means to record a dog's breeding records with an official club. Most collies in North America are family pets. But some still work as herding dogs.

Appearance

Collies have long faces and almond-shaped eyes. Their ears are medium size. They have long tails that curl up at the end.

Collies have long faces and almond-shaped eyes.

Collies are large dogs. Males are 24 to 26 inches (61 to 66 centimeters) tall. Females are 22 to 24 inches (56 to 61 centimeters) tall. Height is measured from the ground to the withers. The withers are the tops of the shoulders. Males weigh 60 to 75 pounds (27 to 34 kilograms). Females weigh 50 to 65 pounds (23 to 29 kilograms).

There are two kinds of collies. They are smooth and rough collies. Smooth collies have short coats. Rough collies have long coats. The dogs that played Lassie were rough collies.

Collie Colors

Collies can have any of four color patterns. These patterns are sable and white, tricolor, blue merle, and white. Colors are the same for smooth and rough collies.

Sable and white is the best-known collie color pattern. Sable and white collies have white markings on the chest, legs, and tail. The dogs that played Lassie were sable and white.

Sable and white collies have white markings on the chest, legs, and tail.

Tricolor collies are mostly black. They have tan markings on the head and legs. They also have white markings on the chest, legs, and tail.

Blue merle collies are gray and black. They have tan markings like tricolor collies. They also have white markings on the chest, legs, and tail.

White collies are mostly white with colored markings. The markings can be sable, tricolor, or blue merle. White collies without any markings may be unhealthy.

Some collies have blazes. A blaze is a white stripe down the middle of an animal's face.

Eye Problems

Some collies are born with eye problems. Breeders do not let collies with serious eye problems have puppies. Breeders do not want these dogs to pass the eye problems on to their puppies.

Some collies have blazes.

A common job for collies is herding.

Collies that have slight eye problems can see well and make good pets. But some dogs' eyes get worse over time. Some collies may even go blind.

Working Collies

Collies do many important jobs. They work as service dogs for people who are disabled. They also serve as police dogs. Some owners and their collies visit people in nursing homes and hospitals. The owners and collies try to cheer up the people.

The most common job for working collies is herding. Collies still make excellent herding dogs. They obey commands well. They are gentle enough not to frighten young animals.

A Collie Story

Collies are well known for being faithful. One collie from Los Angeles, California, proved this. The collie's name was Lassie. Lassie's owners named her for the dog in the stories and movies.

Lassie's family moved to New York in 1952. The family brought Lassie with them. But Lassie did not understand she had a new home. One day Lassie disappeared from her family's yard. Her family could not find her.

Two months later, someone found Lassie in Los Angeles. No one knows for sure how she got there. Many people think she walked all the way.

Chapter 5
Owning a Collie

Collies make great family pets. They get along with children and other pets. Collies are intelligent dogs. They need activities to keep them busy. Collies also need plenty of exercise.

Keeping a Collie
Most owners keep their collies indoors. Collies seem to enjoy the company of people. But collies also need to spend time outdoors. Time outdoors allows collies to get the exercise they need. They can run up to 40 miles (64 kilometers) in a day.

Collies need plenty of exercise.

Owners should keep their collies in fenced areas when the dogs are outside. The areas should provide shelter and shade. Collies need room to run and play. Fences should be at least four feet (1.2 meters) high. Collies can jump over shorter fences.

Owners should walk their collies at least once each day. Collies need more exercise than some dog breeds. Owners who cannot walk their collies regularly should find another person who can.

Feeding a Collie

The best diet for a collie is dog food. Pet stores carry several forms of dog food. The most common forms are dry, semimoist, and canned. Collies can eat any one of these forms.

Adult collies usually eat about one pound (.5 kilograms) or more of dry or semimoist food per day. They may eat about four cans

Many people feed their collies twice each day.

of canned food per day instead. Most people feed their collies twice each day. It is important that owners do not give their collies too much food. Collies that gain too much weight can become unhealthy.

Collies need plenty of water. Owners should make sure their dogs can drink as often as they want. Collies should drink at least three times each day.

Grooming

Owners must be willing to groom their collies. Groom means to brush and clean an animal. Owners should not bathe their collies more than once every two months.

Owners must brush their collies at least once each week. Collies shed much of their fur. Shed means to lose hair or skin. Rough collies' coats can become tangled. Owners can keep their collies' coats healthy by brushing their dogs regularly.

Owners must brush their collies at least once each week.

Owners must check their collies for ticks every day during warm weather. Some ticks carry illnesses. Owners also should check collies for fleas, lice, and mites. These are other small creatures that can live in a dog's fur.

Finding a Collie

People who want collie puppies should contact collie clubs in their areas. These clubs help people find good breeders. Good breeders do not sell collies through pet stores. Most breeders warn people not to buy dogs at pet stores. These dogs often are unhealthy.

Anyone buying a collie from a breeder should ask about the dog's eyes. Breeders can tell new owners how to care for their collie's eyes. Breeders will know whether a dog's parents had eye problems. Good

People who want collie puppies should contact collie clubs in their areas.

breeders take puppies to veterinarians before they sell the dogs. Veterinarians check the puppies' eyes for problems.

Some people buy collies from rescue shelters. Rescue shelters find homes for abandoned dogs. Dogs from rescue shelters usually cost less than breeders' dogs. Some are even free. Many rescued dogs are already trained.

People enjoy their collies for many reasons. Collies are smart, friendly, and beautiful. They are also faithful and brave.

A person who buys a collie from a breeder should ask about the dog's eyes.

Tail

Hindquarters

Hock

Ears

Withers

Muzzle

Chest

Forequarters

Quick Facts about Dogs

Dog Terms

A male dog is called a dog. A female dog is called a bitch. A young dog is a puppy until it is one year old. A newborn puppy is a whelp until it no longer depends on its mother's milk. A family of puppies born at one time is called a litter.

Life History

Origin: All dogs, wolves, coyotes, and dingoes descended from a single wolflike species. Dogs have been friends of people since early times.

Types: There are about 350 different dog breeds. Dogs come in different sizes and colors. Adult dogs weigh from two to 200 pounds (one to 91 kilograms). They stand from six to 36 inches (15 to 91 centimeters) tall.

Reproduction: Dogs mature at six to 18 months. Puppies are born two months after breeding. An average litter is three to six puppies, but litters of 15 or more are possible.

Development: Newborn puppies cannot see or hear. Their ears and eyes open one to two weeks after birth. They try to walk about two weeks after birth. Their teeth begin to come in about three weeks after birth.

Life span: Dogs are fully grown at two years. They may live up to 15 years.

The Dog's Super Senses

Smell: Dogs have a strong sense of smell. Dogs
                use their noses even more than their eyes
                and ears. They recognize people, animals,
                and objects just by smelling them. They
                may recognize smells from long distances.
                They also may remember smells for long
                periods of time.

Hearing: Dogs hear better than people do. Dogs can
                hear noises from long distances. They also
                hear high-pitched sounds that people
                cannot hear.

Sight: Dogs' eyes are on the sides of their heads.
                They can see twice as wide around their
                heads as people can. Some scientists
                believe dogs cannot see colors.

Touch: Dogs enjoy being petted more than almost
                any other animal. They also can feel
                vibrations from approaching trains or the
                earliest stages of earthquakes.

Taste: Dogs cannot taste much. This is partly
                because their sense of smell is so strong
                that it overpowers their taste.

Navigation: Dogs often can find their way through
                crowded streets or across miles of
                wilderness without any guidance. This is
                a special ability that scientists do not
                fully understand.

Words to Know

blaze (BLAYZ)—a white stripe down the middle of an animal's face

groom (GROOM)—to brush and clean an animal

register (REJ-uh-stur)—to record a dog's breeding records with an official club

sable (SAY-buhl)—a shade of brown

shed (SHED)—to lose hair or skin

veterinarian (vet-ur-uh-NER-ee-uhn)—a person trained to treat the sicknesses and injuries of animals

withers (WITH-urs)—the tops of an animal's shoulders

To Learn More

Driscoll, Laura. *All about Dogs and Puppies.*
All Aboard Books. New York: Grosset &
Dunlap, 1998.

Hansen, Ann Larkin. *Dogs.* Popular Pet Care.
Minneapolis: Abdo & Daughters, 1997.

Kallen, Stuart. *Collies.* Edina, Minn.: Abdo &
Daughters, 1998.

Rosen, Michael J. *Kids' Best Field Guide to
Neighborhood Dogs.* New York: Workman,
1993.

You can read articles about collies in *AKC
Gazette, Dog Fancy, Dog World,* and
National Stockdog magazines.

Useful Addresses

American Kennel Club
5580 Centerview Drive
Raleigh, NC 27606

American Working Collie Association
208 Harris Road, FA 1
Bedford Hills, NY 10507

Canadian Kennel Club
89 Skyway Avenue, Suite 100
Etobicoke, ON M9W 6R4
Canada

Collie Club of America
1119 South Fleming Road
Woodstock, IL 60098

Collie Club of Canada
Route 2
Loretto, ON L0G 1L0
Canada

Internet Sites

American Kennel Club
http://www.akc.org

American Working Collie Association
http://www.mother.com/~catoft/awca/

Collie Club of America
http://members.aol.com/CCAWWWSITE/cca/

Lassie Network
http://members.aol.com/LassieNet/

Pet Net
http://www.petnet.com

Index